P9-DEQ-057

Vita Nova

BY

Louise Glück

HELEN M. PLUM MEMORIAL LIBRARY
LOMBARD, ILLINOIS

THE ECCO PRESS
An Imprint of HarperCollins*Publishers*

811
GLY

Special thanks to Meredith Hoppin and Ellen Pinsky.

VITA NOVA. Copyright © 1999 by Louise Glück. All rights reserved. Printed in the United States of America. No part of this book may be used or reproduced in any manner whatsoever without written permission except in the case of brief quotations embodied in critical articles and reviews. For information address HarperCollins Publishers Inc., 10 East 53rd Street, New York, NY 10022.

HarperCollins books may be purchased for educational, business, or sales promotional use. For information please write: Special Markets Department, HarperCollins Publishers Inc., 10 East 53rd Street, New York, NY 10022.

Acknowledgement is made to the editors of the following publications in which some of these poems first appeared: *American Poetry Review, The New Yorker, Slate, Threepenny Review*, and *Yale Review*.

First Ecco paperback edition published 2001.

The Library of Congress has catalogued the hardcover edition as follows:
Glück, Lousie, 1943–
    Vita Nova / Louise Glück—1st ed.
    p. cm.
    ISBN 0-88001-634-5
    I. Title.
PS3557.L8V58 1999
811'54—dc21   98-3730

ISBN 0-06-095795-6 (pbk.)

03 04 ❖/RRD 10 9 8 7 6 5 4 3 2

3 1502 00580 7555

TO
Kathryn Davis
Karen Kennerly
and Ellen Bryant Voigt

TO
Tom and Vera Kreilkamp

CONTENTS

Vita Nova

The master said *You must write what you see.*

But what I see does not move me.

The master answered *Change what you see.*

V I T A   N O V A

You saved me, you should remember me.

The spring of the year; young men buying tickets for the
    ferryboats.
Laughter, because the air is full of apple blossoms.

When I woke up, I realized I was capable of the same
    feeling.

I remember sounds like that from my childhood,
laughter for no cause, simply because the world is
    beautiful,
something like that.

Lugano. Tables under the apple trees.
Deckhands raising and lowering the colored flags.
And by the lake's edge, a young man throws his hat into
    the water;
perhaps his sweetheart has accepted him.

Crucial
sounds or gestures like
a track laid down before the larger themes

and then unused, buried.

Islands in the distance. My mother
holding out a plate of little cakes—

as far as I remember, changed
in no detail, the moment
vivid, intact, having never been
exposed to light, so that I woke elated, at my age
hungry for life, utterly confident—

By the tables, patches of new grass, the pale green
pieced into the dark existing ground.

Surely spring has been returned to me, this time
not as a lover but a messenger of death, yet
it is still spring, it is still meant tenderly.

AUBADE

The world was very large. Then
the world was small. O
very small, small enough
to fit in a brain.

It had no color, it was all
interior space: nothing
got in or out. But time
seeped in anyway, that
was the tragic dimension.

I took time very seriously in those years,
if I remember accurately.

A room with a chair, a window.
A small window, filled with the patterns light makes.
In its emptiness the world

was whole always, not
a chip of something, with
the self at the center.

And at the center of the self,
grief I thought I couldn't survive.

A room with a bed, a table. Flashes
of light on the naked surfaces.

I had two desires: desire
to be safe and desire to feel. As though

the world were making
a decision against white
because it disdained potential
and wanted in its place substance:

panels
of gold where the light struck.
In the window, reddish
leaves of the copper beech tree.

Out of the stasis, facts, objects
blurred or knitted together: somewhere

time stirring, time
crying to be touched, to be
palpable,

the polished wood
shimmering with distinctions—

and then I was once more
a child in the presence of riches
and I didn't know what the riches were made of.

THE QUEEN OF CARTHAGE

Brutal to love,
more brutal to die.
And brutal beyond the reaches of justice
to die of love.

In the end, Dido
summoned her ladies in waiting
that they might see
the harsh destiny inscribed for her by the Fates.

She said, "Aeneas
came to me over the shimmering water;
I asked the Fates
to permit him to return my passion,
even for a short time. What difference
between that and a lifetime: in truth, in such moments,
they are the same, they are both eternity.

I was given a great gift
which I attempted to increase, to prolong.
Aeneas came to me over the water: the beginning
blinded me.

Now the Queen of Carthage
will accept suffering as she accepted favor:
to be noticed by the Fates
is some distinction after all.

Or should one say, to have honored hunger,
since the Fates go by that name also."

THE OPEN GRAVE

My mother made my need,
my father my conscience.
De mortuis nil nisi bonum.

Therefore it will cost me
bitterly to lie,
to prostrate myself
at the edge of a grave.

I say to the earth
be kind to my mother,
now and later.
Save, with your coldness,
the beauty we all envied.

I became an old woman.
I welcomed the dark
I used so to fear.
De mortuis nil nisi bonum.

Interesting how we fall in love:
in my case, absolutely. Absolutely, and, alas, often—
so it was in my youth.
And always with rather boyish men—
unformed, sullen, or shyly kicking the dead leaves:
in the manner of Balanchine.
Nor did I see them as versions of the same thing.
I, with my inflexible Platonism,
my fierce seeing of only one thing at a time:
I ruled against the indefinite article.
And yet, the mistakes of my youth
made me hopeless, because they repeated themselves,
as is commonly true.
But in you I felt something beyond the archetype—
a true expansiveness, a buoyance and love of the earth
utterly alien to my nature. To my credit,
I blessed my good fortune in you.
Blessed it absolutely, in the manner of those years.
And you in your wisdom and cruelty
gradually taught me the meaninglessness of that term.

THE BURNING HEART

"... No sadness
is greater than in misery to rehearse
memories of joy. ..."

Ask her if she regrets anything.

I was
promised to another—
I lived with someone.
You forget these things when you're touched.

Ask her how he touched her.

His gaze touched me
before his hands touched me.

Ask her how he touched her.

I didn't ask for anything;
everything was given.

Ask her what she remembers.

We were hauled into the underworld.

I thought
we were not responsible
any more than we were responsible
for being alive. I was
a young girl, rarely subject to censure:

then a pariah. Did I change that much
from one day to the next?
If I didn't change, wasn't my action
in the character of that young girl?

Ask her what she remembers.

I noticed nothing. I noticed
I was trembling.

Ask her if the fire hurts.

I remember
we were together.
And gradually I understood
that though neither of us ever moved
we were not together but profoundly separate.

Ask her if the fire hurts.

You expect to live forever with your husband
in fire more durable than the world.
I suppose this wish was granted,
where we are now being both
fire and eternity.

Do you regret your life?

Even before I was touched, I belonged to you;
you had only to look at me.

ROMAN STUDY

He felt at first
he should have been born
to Aphrodite, not Venus,
that too little was left to do,
to accomplish, after the Greeks.

And he resented light,
to which Greece has
the greatest claim.

He cursed his mother
(privately, discreetly),
she who could have arranged all of this.

And then it occurred to him
to examine these responses
in which, finally, he recognized
a new species of thought entirely,
more worldly, more ambitious
and politic, in what we now call
human terms.

And the longer he thought
the more he experienced
faint contempt for the Greeks,
for their austerity, the eerie
balance of even the great tragedies—
thrilling at first, then
faintly predictable, routine.

And the longer he thought
the more plain to him how much
still remained to be experienced,
and written down, a material world heretofore
hardly dignified.

And he recognized in exactly this reasoning
the scope and trajectory of his own
watchful nature.

THE NEW LIFE

I slept the sleep of the just,
later the sleep of the unborn
who come into the world
guilty of many crimes.
And what these crimes are
nobody knows at the beginning.
Only after many years does one know.
Only after long life is one prepared
to read the equation.

I begin now to perceive
the nature of my soul, the soul
I inhabit as punishment.
Inflexible, even in hunger.

I have been in my other lives
too hasty, too eager,
my haste a source of pain in the world.
Swaggering as a tyrant swaggers;
for all my amorousness,
cold at heart, in the manner of the superficial.

I slept the sleep of the just;
I lived the life of a criminal
slowly repaying an impossible debt.
And I died having answered for
one species of ruthlessness.

FORMAGGIO

The world
was whole because
it shattered. When it shattered,
then we knew what it was.

It never healed itself.
But in the deep fissures, smaller worlds appeared:
it was a good thing that human beings made them;
human beings know what they need,
better than any god.

On Huron Avenue they became
a block of stores; they became
Fishmonger, Formaggio. Whatever
they were or sold, they were
alike in their function: they were
visions of safety. Like
a resting place. The salespeople
were like parents; they appeared
to live there. On the whole,
kinder than parents.

Tributaries
feeding into a large river: I had
many lives. In the provisional world,
I stood where the fruit was,
flats of cherries, clementines,
under Hallie's flowers.

I had many lives. Feeding
into a river, the river
feeding into a great ocean. If the self
becomes invisible has it disappeared?

I thrived. I lived
not completely alone, alone
but not completely, strangers
surging around me.

That's what the sea is:
we exist in secret.

I had lives before this, stems
of a spray of flowers: they became
one thing, held by a ribbon at the center, a ribbon
visible under the hand. Above the hand,
the branching future, stems
ending in flowers. And the gripped fist—
that would be the self in the present.

TIMOR MORTIS

Why are you afraid?

A man in a top hat passed under the bedroom window.
I couldn't have been
more than four at the time.

It was a dream: I saw him
when I was high up, where I should have been
safe from him.

Do you remember your childhood?

When the dream ended
terror remained. I lay in my bed—
my crib maybe.

I dreamed I was kidnapped. That means
I knew what love was,
how it places the soul in jeopardy.
I knew. I substituted my body.

But you were hostage?

I was afraid of love, of being taken away.
Everyone afraid of love is afraid of death.

I pretended indifference
even in the presence of love, in the presence of hunger.
And the more deeply I felt
the less able I was to respond.

Do you remember your childhood?

I understood that the magnitude of these gifts
was balanced by the scope of my rejection.

Do you remember your childhood?

I lay in the forest.
Still, more still than any living creature.
Watching the sun rise.

And I remember once my mother turning away from me
in great anger. Or perhaps it was grief.
Because for all she had given me,
for all her love, I failed to show gratitude.
And I made no sign of understanding.

For which I was never forgiven.

LUTE SONG

No one wants to be the muse;
in the end, everyone wants to be Orpheus.

Valiantly reconstructed
(out of terror and pain)
and then overwhelmingly beautiful;

restoring, ultimately,
not Eurydice, the lamented one,
but the ardent
spirit of Orpheus, made present

not as a human being, rather
as pure soul rendered
detached, immortal,
through deflected narcissism.

I made a harp of disaster
to perpetuate the beauty of my last love.
Yet my anguish, such as it is,
remains the struggle for form

and my dreams, if I speak openly,
less the wish to be remembered
than the wish to survive,
which is, I believe, the deepest human wish.

ORFEO

"J'ai perdu mon Eurydice. . . ."

I have lost my Eurydice,
I have lost my lover,
and suddenly I am speaking French
and it seems to me I have never been in better voice;
it seems these songs
are songs of a high order.

And it seems one is somehow expected to apologize
for being an artist,
as though it were not entirely human to notice these fine
        points.
And who knows, perhaps the gods never spoke to me in
        Dis,
never singled me out,
perhaps it was all illusion.

O Eurydice, you who married me for my singing,
why do you turn on me, wanting human comfort?
Who knows what you'll tell the furies
when you see them again.

Tell them I have lost my beloved;
I am completely alone now.
Tell them there is no music like this
without real grief.

In Dis, I sang to them; they will remember me.

DESCENT TO THE VALLEY

I found the years of the climb upward
difficult, filled with anxiety.
I didn't doubt my capacities:
rather, as I moved toward it,
I feared the future, the shape of which
I perceived. I saw
the shape of a human life:
on the one side, always upward and forward
into the light; on the other side,
downward into the mists of uncertainty.
All eagerness undermined by knowledge.

I have found it otherwise.
The light of the pinnacle, the light that was,
theoretically, the goal of the climb,
proves to have been poignantly abstract:
my mind, in its ascent,
was entirely given over to detail, never
perception of form; my eyes
nervously attending to footing.

How sweet my life now
in its descent to the valley,
the valley itself not mist-covered
but fertile and tranquil.
So that for the first time I find myself
able to look ahead, able to look at the world,
even to move toward it.

THE GARMENT

My soul dried up.
Like a soul cast into fire, but not completely,
not to annihilation. Parched,
it continued. Brittle,
not from solitude but from mistrust,
the aftermath of violence.

Spirit, invited to leave the body,
to stand exposed a moment,
trembling, as before
your presentation to the divine—
spirit lured out of solitude
by the promise of grace,
how will you ever again believe
the love of another being?

My soul withered and shrank.
The body became for it too large a garment.

And when hope was returned to me
it was another hope entirely.

CONDO

I lived in a tree. The dream specified
pine, as though it thought I needed
prompting to keep mourning. I hate
when your own dreams treat you as stupid.

Inside, it was
my apartment in Plainfield, twenty years ago,
except I'd added a commercial stove.
Deep-rooted

passion for the second floor! Just because
the past is longer than the future
doesn't mean there is no future.

The dream confused them, mistaking
one for the other: repeated

scenes of the gutted house—Vera was there,
talking about the light.
And certainly there was a lot of light, since
there were no walls.

I thought: this is where the bed would be,
where it was in Plainfield.
And deep serenity flooded through me,
such as you feel when the world can't touch you.
Beyond the invisible bed, light
of late summer in the little street,
between flickering ash trees.

Which the dream changed, adding, you could say,
a dimension of hope. It was
a beautiful dream, my life was small and sweet, the world
broadly visible because remote.

The dream showed me how to have it again
by being safe from it. It showed me
sleeping in my old bed, first stars
shining through bare ash trees.

I have been lifted and carried far away
into a luminous city. Is this what having means,
to look down on? Or is this dreaming still?
I was right, wasn't I, choosing
against the ground?

IMMORTAL LOVE

Like a door
the body opened and
the soul looked out.
Timidly at first, then
less timidly
until it was safe.
Then in hunger it ventured.
Then in brazen hunger,
then at the invitation
of any desire.

Promiscuous one, how will you find
god now? How will you
ascertain the divine?
Even in the garden you were told
to live in the body, not
outside it, and suffer in it
if that comes to be necessary.
How will god find you
if you are never in one place
long enough, never
in the home he gave you?

Or do you believe
you have no home, since god
never meant to contain you?

EARTHLY LOVE

Conventions of the time
held them together.
It was a period
(very long) in which
the heart once given freely
was required, as a formal gesture,
to forfeit liberty: a consecration
at once moving and hopelessly doomed.

As to ourselves:
fortunately we diverged
from these requirements,
as I reminded myself
when my life shattered.
So that what we had for so long
was, more or less,
voluntary, alive.
And only long afterward
did I begin to think otherwise.

We are all human—
we protect ourselves
as well as we can
even to the point of denying
clarity, the point
of self-deception. As in
the consecration to which I alluded.

And yet, within this deception,
true happiness occurred.

So that I believe I would
repeat these errors exactly.
Nor does it seem to me
crucial to know
whether or not such happiness
is built on illusion:
it has its own reality.
And in either case, it will end.

EURYDICE

Eurydice went back to hell.
What was difficult
was the travel, which,
on arrival, is forgotten.

Transition
is difficult.
And moving between two worlds
especially so;
the tension is very great.

A passage
filled with regret, with longing,
to which we have, in the world,
some slight access or memory.

Only for a moment
when the dark of the underworld
settled around her again
(gentle, respectful),
only for a moment could
an image of earth's beauty
reach her again, beauty
for which she grieved.

But to live with human faithlessness
is another matter.

CASTILE

Orange blossoms blowing over Castile
children begging for coins

I met my love under an orange tree
or was it an acacia tree
or was he not my love?

I read this, then I dreamed this:
can waking take back what happened to me?
Bells of San Miguel
ringing in the distance
his hair in the shadows blond-white

I dreamed this,
does that mean it didn't happen?
Does it have to happen in the world to be real?

I dreamed everything, the story
became my story:

he lay beside me,
my hand grazed the skin of his shoulder

Mid-day, then early evening:
in the distance, the sound of a train

But it was not the world:
in the world, a thing happens finally, absolutely,
the mind cannot reverse it.

Castile: nuns walking in pairs through the dark garden.
Outside the walls of the Holy Angels
children begging for coins

When I woke I was crying,
has that no reality?

I met my love under an orange tree:
I have forgotten
only the facts, not the inference—
there were children somewhere, crying, begging for coins

I dreamed everything, I gave myself
completely and for all time

And the train returned us
first to Madrid
then to the Basque country

MUTABLE EARTH

Are you healed or do you only think you're healed?

I told myself
from nothing
nothing could be taken away.

But can you love anyone yet?

When I feel safe, I can love.

But will you touch anyone?

I told myself
if I had nothing
the world couldn't touch me.

In the bathtub, I examine my body.
We're supposed to do that.

And your face too?
Your face in the mirror?

I was vigilant: when I touched myself
I didn't feel anything.

Were you safe then?

I was never safe, even when I was most hidden.
Even then I was waiting.

So you couldn't protect yourself?

The absolute
erodes; the boundary, the wall
around the self erodes.
If I was waiting I had been
invaded by time.

But do you think you're free?

I think I recognize the patterns of my nature.

But do you think you're free?

I had nothing
and I was still changed.
Like a costume, my numbness
was taken away. Then
hunger was added.

THE WINGED HORSE

Here is my horse Abstraction,
silver-white, color of the page,
of the unwritten.

Come, Abstraction,
by Will out of Demonic Ambition:
carry me lightly into the regions of the immortal.

I am weary of my other mount,
by Instinct out of Reality,
color of dust, of disappointment,
notwithstanding
the saddle that went with him
and the bronze spurs, the bit
of indestructible metal.

I am weary of the world's gifts, the world's
stipulated limits.

And I am weary of being opposed
and weary of being constantly contradicted by the
        material, as by
a massive wall where all I say can be
checked up on.

Then come, Abstraction,
take me where you have taken so many others,
far from here, to the void, the star pasture.

Bear me quickly,
Dream out of Blind Hope.

EARTHLY TERROR

I stood at the gate of a rich city.
I had everything the gods required;
I was ready; the burdens
of preparation had been long.
And the moment was the right moment,
the moment assigned to me.

Why were you afraid?

The moment was the right moment;
response must be ready.
On my lips,
the words trembled that were
the right words. Trembled—

and I knew that if I failed to answer
quickly enough, I would be turned away.

Even the goddess of love
fights for her children, her vanity
notwithstanding: more than other heroes,
Aeneas flourished; even the road back upward from hell
was simplified. And the sacrifice of love
less painful than for the other heroes.
His mind was clear: even as he endured sacrifice,
he saw its practical purpose. His mind was clear,
and in its clarity, fortified against despair,
even as grief made more human a heart
that might otherwise have seemed immutable. And beauty
ran in his veins: he had no need
for more of it. He conceded to other visions
the worlds of art and science, those paths that lead
only to torment, and instead gathered
the diverse populations of earth
into an empire, a conception
of justice through submission, an intention "to spare the humble
and to crush the proud": subjective,
necessarily, as judgments necessarily are.
Beauty ran in his veins; he had no need for more of it.
That and his taste for empire:
that much can be verified.

EVENING PRAYERS

I believe my sin
to be entirely common:
the request for help
masking request for favor
and the plea for pity
thinly veiling complaint.

So little at peace in the spring evening,
I pray for strength, for direction,
but I also ask
to survive my illness
(the immediate one)—never mind
anything in the future.
I make this a special point,
this unconcern for the future,
also the courage I will have acquired by then
to meet my suffering alone
but with heightened fortitude.

Tonight, in my unhappiness,
I wonder what qualities this presumes
in the one who listens.
And as the breeze stirs
the leaves of the little birch tree,
I construct a presence
wholly skeptical and wholly tender,
thus incapable of surprise.

I believe my sin is common, therefore
intended; I can feel

the leaves stir, sometimes
with words, sometimes without,
as though the highest form of pity
could be irony.

Bedtime, they whisper.
Time to begin lying.

RELIC

Where would I be without my sorrow,
sorrow of my beloved's making,
without some sign of him, this song
of all gifts the most lasting?

How would you like to die
while Orpheus was singing?
A long death; all the way to Dis
I heard him.

Torment of earth
Torment of mortal passion—

I think sometimes
too much is asked of us;
I think sometimes
our consolations are the costliest thing.

All the way to Dis
I heard my husband singing,
much as you now hear me.
Perhaps it was better that way,
my love fresh in my head
even at the moment of death.

Not the first response—
that was terror—
but the last.

NEST

A bird was making its nest.
In the dream, I watched it closely:
in my life, I was trying to be
a witness not a theorist.

The place you begin doesn't determine
the place you end: the bird

took what it found in the yard,
its base materials, nervously
scanning the bare yard in early spring;
in debris by the south wall pushing
a few twigs with its beak.

Image
of loneliness: the small creature
coming up with nothing. Then
dry twigs. Carrying, one by one,
the twigs to the hideout.
Which is all it was then.

It took what there was:
the available material. Spirit
wasn't enough.

And then it wove like the first Penelope
but toward a different end.
How did it weave? It weaved,
carefully but hopelessly, the few twigs

with any suppleness, any flexibility,
choosing these over the brittle, the recalcitrant.

Early spring, late desolation.
The bird circled the bare yard making
efforts to survive
on what remained to it.

It had its task:
to imagine the future. Steadily flying around,
patiently bearing small twigs to the solitude
of the exposed tree in the steady coldness
of the outside world.

I had nothing to build with.
It was winter: I couldn't imagine
anything but the past. I couldn't even
imagine the past, if it came to that.

And I didn't know how I came here.
Everyone else much farther along.
I was back at the beginning
at a time in life we can't remember beginnings.

The bird
collected twigs in the apple tree, relating
each addition to existing mass.
But when was there suddenly *mass?*

It took what it found after the others
were finished.
The same materials—why should it matter
to be finished last? The same materials, the same
limited good. Brown twigs,
broken and fallen. And in one,
a length of yellow wool.

Then it was spring and I was inexplicably happy.
I knew where I was: on Broadway with my bag of groceries.
Spring fruit in the stores: first
cherries at Formaggio. Forsythia
beginning.

First I was at peace.
Then I was contented, satisfied.
And then flashes of joy.
And the season changed—for all of us,
of course.

And as I peered out my mind grew sharper.
And I remember accurately
the sequence of my responses,
my eyes fixing on each thing
from the shelter of the hidden self:

first, *I love it.*
Then, *I can use it.*

ELLSWORTH AVENUE

      Spring
descended. Or should one say
rose? Should one say rose up?
At the Butlers' house,
witch hazel in bloom.

So it would have been
late February.

Pale
yellow of the new year,
unpracticed color. Sheen
of ice over the dull ground.

I thought: *stop now,* meaning
stop here.
Speaking of my life.

The spring of the year: yellow-
green of forsythia, the Commons
planted with new grass—

the new
protected always, the new thing
given its explicit shield, its metal
plaque of language, bordered
with white rope.

Because we wish it to live,

a pale green
hemming the dark existing shapes.

Late
winter sun. Or spring?
The spring sun
so early? Screened
by dense forsythia. I looked
directly into it or almost into it—

Across the street, a small boy
threw his hat into the air: the new

ascending always, the fresh
unsteady colors climbing and rising,
alternating
blue and gold:

Ellsworth Avenue.
A striped
abstraction of the human head
triumphant over dead shrubs.

     Spring
descended. Or should one say
rose up again? Or should one say
broke from earth?

INFERNO

Why did you move away?

I walked out of the fire alive;
how can that be?

How much was lost?

Nothing was lost: it was all
destroyed. Destruction
is the result of action.

Was there a real fire?

I remember going back into the house twenty years ago,
trying to save what we could.
Porcelain and so on. The smell of smoke
on everything.

In my dream, I built a funeral pyre.
For myself, you understand.
I thought I had suffered enough.

I thought this was the end of my body: fire
seemed the right end for hunger;
they were the same thing.

And yet you didn't die?

It was a dream; I thought I was going home.

I remember telling myself
it wouldn't work; I remember thinking
my soul was too stubborn to die.
I thought soul was the same as consciousness—
probably everyone thinks that.

Why did you move away?

I woke up in another world.
As simple as that.

Why did you move away?

The world changed. I walked out of the fire
into a different world—maybe
the world of the dead, for all I know.
Not the end of need but need
raised to the highest power.

SEIZURE

You saved me, you should remember me.

You came to me; twice
I saw you in the garden.
When I woke I was on the ground.

I didn't know who I was anymore;
I didn't know what trees were.

Twice in the garden; many times
before that. Why should it be
kept secret?

The raspberries were very thick;
I hadn't pruned them, I hadn't weeded anything.

I didn't know where I was.
Only: there was a fire near me—no,
above me. In the distance,
the sound of a river.

It was never focus that was missing,
it was meaning.

There was a crown,
a circle over my head.
My hands were covered with dirt,
not from labor.

Why should I lie: that life
is over now.
Why shouldn't I
use what I know?

You changed me, you should remember me.

I remember I had gone out
to walk in the garden. As before into
the streets of the city, into
the bedroom of that first apartment.

And yes, I was alone;
how could I not be?

The Mystery

I became a creature of light.
I sat in a driveway in California;
the roses were hydrant-color; a baby
rolled by in its yellow stroller, making
bubbling fishlike sounds.

I sat in a folding chair
reading Nero Wolfe for the twentieth time,
a mystery that has become restful.
I know who the innocent are; I have acquired in some
        measure
the genius of the master, in whose supple mind
time moves in two directions: backward
from the act to the motive
and forward to just resolution.

Fearless heart, never tremble again:
the only shadow is the narrow palm's
that cannot enclose you absolutely.
Not like the shadows of the east.

My life took me many places,
many of them very dark.
It took me without my volition,
pushing me from behind,
from one world to another, like
the fishlike baby.
And it was all entirely arbitrary,
without discernible form.

The passionate threats and questions,
the old search for justice,
must have been entirely deluded.

And yet I saw amazing things.
I became almost radiant at the end;
I carried my book everywhere,
like an eager student
clinging to these simple mysteries

so that I might silence in myself
the last accusations:

Who are you and what is your purpose?

LAMENT

A terrible thing is happening—my love
is dying again, my love who has died already:
died and been mourned. And music continues,
music of separation: the trees
become instruments.

How cruel the earth, the willows shimmering,
the birches bending and sighing.
How cruel, how profoundly tender.

My love is dying; my love
not only a person, but an idea, a life.

What will I live for?
Where will I find him again
if not in grief, dark wood
from which the lute is made.

Once is enough. Once is enough
to say goodbye on earth.
And to grieve, that too, of course.
Once is enough to say goodbye forever.

The willows shimmer by the stone fountain,
paths of flowers abutting.

Once is enough: why is he living again?
And so briefly, and only in dream.

My love is dying; parting has started again.
And through the veils of the willows
sunlight rising and glowing,
not the light we knew.
And the birds singing again, even the mourning dove.

Ah, I have sung this song. By the stone fountain
the willows are singing again
with unspeakable tenderness, trailing their leaves
in the radiant water.

Clearly they know, they know. He is dying again,
and the world also. Dying the rest of my life,
so I believe.

In the splitting up dream
we were fighting over who would keep
the dog,
Blizzard. You tell me
what that name means. He was
a cross between
something big and fluffy
and a dachshund. Does this have to be
the male and female
genitalia? Poor Blizzard,
why was he a dog? He barely touched
the hummus in his dogfood dish.
Then there was something else,
a sound. Like
gravel being moved. Or sand?
The sands of time? Then it was
Erica with her maracas,
like the sands of time
personified. Who will
explain this to
the dog? Blizzard,
Daddy needs you; Daddy's heart is empty,
not because he's leaving Mommy but because
the kind of love he wants Mommy
doesn't have, Mommy's
too ironic—Mommy wouldn't do
the rhumba in the driveway. Or
is this wrong. Supposing
I'm the dog, as in

my child-self, unconsolable because
completely pre-verbal? With
anorexia! O Blizzard,
be a brave dog—this is
all material; you'll wake up
in a different world,
you will eat again, you will grow up into a poet!
Life is very weird, no matter how it ends,
very filled with dreams. Never
will I forget your face, your frantic human eyes
swollen with tears.
I thought my life was over and my heart was broken.
Then I moved to Cambridge.